Super Easy

Mediterranean Diet

Cookbook 2021

Start Cooking with Super Easy
Mediterranean Diet Recipes for Eat
Healthy Foods and Lose Weight without
Sacrificing Taste!

Jim Smith

Table of Contents

question by the reader will render any resulting actions solely under their purview. There are no scenarios in which the publisher or the original author of this work can be in any fashion deemed liable for any hardship or damages that may befall them after undertaking information described herein.

Additionally, the information in the following pages is intended only for informational purposes and should thus be thought of as universal. As befitting its nature, it is presented without assurance regarding its prolonged validity or interim quality. Trademarks that are mentioned are done without written consent and can in no way be considered an endorsement from the trademark holder.

INTRODUCTION

The Mediterranean eating regimen is a way of life. It's a method of eating so as to carry on with a full and solid life. When following along these lines of eating you'll get in shape, yet you'll likewise reinforce your heart and give your body all the best possible supplements important to carry on with a long and profitable life. Individuals following the Mediterranean eating regimen have been connected to a lower danger of Alzheimer's malady and malignancy, better generally speaking cardiovascular wellbeing, and an all-inclusive life expectancy. A Mediterranean style eating regimen is joined by a way of life. The way of life has many things that complete the eating routine. It incorporates a lot of exercise, not smoking, drinking in moderation, and having an enthusiasm for your family and life. This is a genuinely effective methodology for keeping up a solid life. The basic premise of this eating routine is that you eat a considerable measure of vegetables, fruits, cereals, nuts, and whole grains. You eat fish or meat scarcely. The omission of meat lessens your hazard of malignancy. You eat some bread. These are a few of the fundamental things that this eating regimen is all about.

The other portion of the Mediterranean eating regimen is the social component. You eat with your loved ones, family, and companions. You profit by the nourishment that you get and you savor your life. You eat inwardly back and center. Your family and companions appreciate it and they likewise figure out how to appreciate it. You meet a few people who are like-minded and you progress toward becoming a family. You get to appreciate your life since you're living it to the most astounding extent conceivable.

You can't take in the Mediterranean eating routine truly unless you be mindful of the exercise, the moderation, and being with the individuals who make it an occurrence to appreciate life. This is for the most part an approach of life. In the event that you need to accomplish the full advantages let this be the best way you choose to live your life. For the most part the general public who are doing it go to the gatherings that are as a rule home based. They have fun, they do things under the sun, and they do issues with their families and clan. They make a decent attempt to live in that sort of setting as opposed to the conventional social environment that a great many people are ordinarily in.

The last piece of the Mediterranean eating regimen is the way of life. One of the things that can be exceptionally harming is the way that you don't chat with your folks sufficiently. You don't get yourself the chance to hear your companions talk about the things that they appreciate, the things that they comprehend, and the things that they be in a position to do for themselves. They appreciate listening to you talk approximately the things that you appreciate, the things that you comprehend, and the things that you can do for yourself. Planning an occasion to get together so you can talk with your companions about your most loved subjects and every one of the underlying intricacies of your life is an essential piece on the way to accomplish the full advantages of the Mediterranean eating routine.

DESSERT RECIPES

Caramelized Apples with Yogurt

Preparation Time: 14 minutes

Cooking Time: 9 minutes

Servings: 4

Size/ Portion: 1 cup

Ingredients:

- 1/2 cup Greek yogurt

- 2 tbsp. toasted, chopped walnuts

- 1/4 cup heavy cream

- 1 tbsp. sugar

- 1/2 tbsp. honey

- 1 tbsp. unsalted butter

- 1 apple

- a pinch of ground cinnamon

Directions:

1. Take a bowl and add the yogurt, honey, and cream. Next, beat it with a hand blender or a whisk. Beat it until the mixture forms peaks and has thickened.
2. Place a large skillet on medium heat and warm the butter.
3. Add 21 grams of sugar and the apples in to the pan and mix it well.
4. Cook the apples for five to seven minutes while occasionally stirring, so it doesn't stick.

5. Once the apples soften, sprinkle the cinnamon and the remaining sugar on them.
6. Cook for 2 more minutes before removing from the heat.
7. Wait for the apples to appear warm.
8. Serve the whipped yogurt topped with apples and almonds.

Nutrition: 315 Calories 6.4g Protein 22g Fat

Ricotta Brulee

Preparation Time: 7 minutes

Cooking Time: 14 minutes

Servings: 4

Size/ portion: 1 bowl

Ingredients:

- fresh raspberries
- 1 cup whole milk ricotta cheese
- 1 tbsp. granulated sugar
- 1/2 tsp. finely grated lemon zest
- 1 tbsp. honey

Directions:

1. Take a large bowl, stir in the lemon zest, ricotta, and honey.

2. Combine the ingredients well.

3. Place four ramekins and divide the batter among them.

4. Add sugar on top if you don't have a kitchen torch.

5. Add all of the ramekins on a baking sheet and place it on the oven rack.

6. Keep the rack on the highest level and turn the broiler on.

7. Once the ricotta is golden-brown and starts to bubble, turn the oven off.

8. Top with raspberries once it has cooled down. Serve it cold.

Nutrition: 254 Calories 12.8g Protein 14.7g Fat

Chocolate Quinoa Bars

Preparation Time: 19 minutes

Cooking Time: 6 minutes

Servings: 10

Size/ portion: 2 bars

Ingredients:

- 1/4 tsp. vanilla

- 2 oz. semi-sweet chocolate

- 1/2 cup dry quinoa

- 1/2 tbsp. powdered peanut butter

Peanut Butter Drizzle:

- 1 tbsp. water

- 9 tsp. powdered peanut butter

Directions:

1. Place a large pot on medium heat.

2. Once the pot is hot, add the quinoa, 45 grams at a time.

3. Stir the quinoa occasionally, until you start hearing it pop.

4. Once the popping starts, stir continuously for a minute.

5. Once you see that the quinoa has popped, place it in a small bowl.

6. Set up a double boiler and melt your chocolate.

7. Take a large bowl and add the chocolate, peanut butter powder, vanilla, and quinoa.

8. Mix it well to combine.

9. Place a parchment paper on the baking sheet.

10. Spread the chocolate batter across, making it around half an inch thick.

11. Mix together water and peanut butter to make the drizzle, and then drizzle it over the chocolate.

12. Swirl it around with a fork.

13. Refrigerate for it to set, and then slice them into small bars.

Nutrition: 170 Calories 4g Protein 8g Fat

Almond Honey Ricotta Spread

Preparation Time: 7 minutes

Cooking Time: 15 minutes

Servings: 3

Size/ Portion: 2 tablespoons

Ingredients:

- 1/2 cup whole milk ricotta

- orange zest

- 1/4 cup sliced almonds

- 1/8 tsp. almond extract

- 1/2 tsp. honey

- sliced peaches

- honey to drizzle

Directions:

1. Take a medium bowl, and combine almonds, almond extract and ricotta.
2. Once you have stirred it well, place it in a bowl to serve.
3. Sprinkle with sliced almonds and drizzle some honey on the ricotta.
4. Spread a tablespoon of the spread to your choice of bread, top it with some honey and sliced peaches.

Nutrition: 199 Calories 8.5g Protein 12g Fat

Apricot Energy Bites

Preparation Time: 16 minutes

Cooking Time: 0 minute

Servings: 10

Size/ Portion: 2 balls

Ingredients:

- 1 cup unsalted raw cashew nuts
- 1/4 tsp. ground ginger
- 1/2 cup dried apricots
- 2 3/4 tbsp. shredded, unsweetened coconut
- 2 tbsp. chopped dates
- 1 tsp. orange zest
- 1 tsp. lemon zest
- 1/4 tsp. cinnamon
- salt to taste

Directions:

1. Grind apricots, coconut, dates and cashew nuts in a processor.
2. Pulse until all a crumbly mixture has formed.
3. Add the spices, salt and citrus zest in the mixture.
4. Pulse it again to mix well.
5. Process the batter on high till it sticks together.
6. Take a dish or a tray and line it with parchment paper.

7. Shape the balls in your palm, make around 20 balls.
8. Keep in the refrigerator. Serve as needed.

Nutrition: 102 Calories 2g Protein 6g Fat

Pistachio Snack Bars

Preparation Time: 17 minutes

Cooking Time: 0 minute

Servings: 4

Size/ portion: 2 bars

Ingredients:

- 10 pitted dates

- 1/2 tsp. vanilla extract

- 1 tbsp. pistachio butter

- 10 tbsp. roasted, salted pistachios

- 1/2 cup rolled oats, old fashioned

- 2 tbsp. unsweetened, applesauce

Directions:

1. Grind dates until pureed, in a processor.

2. Add the oats and 123 grams of pistachios and pulse a few times for 15 seconds each time.

3. Once there's a coarse and crumbly consistency, add the pistachio butter, vanilla extract, and applesauce until the dough becomes sticky.

4. Line a standard pan with parchment paper.

5. Place the dough on the pan, place another parchment paper on top, and press it down to evenly flatten the dough.

6. Sprinkle the remaining pistachios after removing the parchment paper.

7. Place the paper on top of the dough again and freeze for a while before cutting it into 8 equal bars.

Nutrition: 220 Calories 6g Protein 12g Fat

Oat Berry Smoothie

Preparation Time: 4 minutes

Cooking Time: 0 minute

Servings: 2

Size/ Portion: 1 glass

Ingredients:

- 1/2 cup frozen berries
- 1/2 cup Greek yogurt
- milk
- 4 1/2 tbsp. oats
- 1 tsp. honey

Directions:

1. Blend the berries, milk, and yogurt together until it's smooth.
2. Mix in the porridge oats, pour in a glass once it's mixed well, and drizzle some honey on top.

Nutrition: 295 Calories 18g Protein 5g Fat

SIDE DISHES AND SAUCES

Chili Veggie Mix

Preparation Time: 30 Minutes

Cooking Time: 3 Hours

Servings: 6

Ingredients:

- 1 cup cauliflower, chopped
- 1 cup broccoli, chopped
- 1 cup green peas
- 4 oz. asparagus, chopped
- One teaspoon salt
- One tablespoon lemon juice
- One teaspoon avocado oil
- ½ teaspoon chili flakes
- 2 cups water for the steamer

Directions:

1. Pour water into the pan and wait for it to boil.
2. Insert the steamer in the saucepan.
3. After this, place the vegetables in the steamer and close the lid.
4. Cook the vegetables for 10 minutes or until they are tender.
5. Then transfer the cooked vegetables to the mixing bowl.
6. In the shallow bowl, whisk together salt, lemon juice, avocado oil, and chili flakes.
7. Sprinkle the cooked vegetables with oil mixture and shake well.
8. Transfer the meat to the serving plates.

Nutrition: Calories 34 Fat 0.3 Fiber 2.5 Carbs 6.2 Protein 2.5

Sautéed Collard Greens

Preparation Time: 5 Minutes

Cooking Time: 45 Minutes

Servings: 6

Ingredients:

- 1-pound fresh collard greens, cut into 2-inch pieces
- One pinch of red pepper flakes
- 3 cups chicken broth
- One teaspoon pepper
- One teaspoon salt
- Two cloves garlic, minced
- One large onion, chopped
- Three slices of bacon
- One tablespoon olive oil

Directions:

1. Using a large skillet, heat oil on medium-high heat. Sauté bacon until crisp. Remove it from the pan and crumble it once cooled. Set it aside.
2. Using the same pan, sauté onion, and cook until tender. Add garlic until aromatic. Put the collard greens and cook until they start to wilt.
3. Pour in the chicken broth and season with pepper, salt, and red pepper flakes. Lessen the heat to low, then simmer for 45 minutes.

Nutrition: Calories per **Serving:** 20 Carbs: 3.0g Protein: 1.0g Fat: 1.0g

Garlic Basil Zucchini

Preparation Time: 5 Minutes

Cooking Time: 8 Minutes

Servings: 4

Ingredients:

- 14 oz. zucchini, sliced
- 1/4 cup fresh basil, chopped
- 1/2 tsp red pepper flakes
- 14 oz. can tomato, chopped
- 1 tsp garlic, minced
- 1/2 onion, chopped
- 1/4 cup feta cheese, crumbled
- 1 tbsp. olive oil
- Salt

Directions:

1. Add oil into the inner pot of the instant pot and set the pot on sauté mode.
2. Add onion and garlic and sauté for minutes.
3. Add remaining ingredients except for feta cheese and stir well.
4. Seal pot with lid and cook on high for 6 minutes.
5. Once done, allow to release pressure naturally. Remove lid.
6. Top with feta cheese and serve.

Nutrition: Calories 99 Fat 5.7 g Carbohydrates 10.4 g Sugar 6.1 g Protein 3.7 g Cholesterol 8 mg

Asian Steamed Broccoli

Preparation Time: 5 Minutes

Cooking Time: 10 Minutes

Servings: 6

Ingredients:

- Three tablespoons olive oil
- Three cloves of garlic, minced
- Two tablespoons ginger, sliced
- Two heads of broccoli, cut into florets
- Three tablespoons sesame oil
- Two tablespoons coconut aminos

Directions:

1. Heat olive oil in a pot.
2. Sauté the garlic and ginger until fragrant, around 3 minutes.
3. Add the rest of the ingredients.
4. Stir fry until tender, around 7 minutes.

Nutrition: Calories per **Serving:** 128 Carbs: 1.4g Protein: 0.6g Fat: 13.6g

Chinese Soy Eggplant

Preparation Time: 5 Minutes

Cooking Time: 10 Minutes

Servings: 2

Ingredients:

- Four tablespoons coconut oil
- Two eggplants, sliced into 3-inch in length
- Four cloves of garlic, minced
- One onion, chopped
- One teaspoon ginger, grated
- ¼ cup coconut aminos
- One teaspoon lemon juice, freshly squeezed

Directions:

1. Heat oil in a pot.
2. Pan-fry the eggplants for minutes on all sides.
3. Add the garlic and onions until fragrant, around minutes.
4. Stir in the ginger, coconut aminos, and lemon juice.
5. Add a ½ cup of water and let it simmer. Cook until eggplant is tender.

Nutrition: Calories per **Serving:** 409 Carbs: 40.8g Protein: 6.6g Fat: 28.3g

Cauliflower Mash

Preparation Time: 5 Minutes

Cooking Time: 0 Minutes

Servings: 2

Ingredients:

- Crushed red pepper to taste
- 1 tsp fresh thyme
- 2 tsp chopped chives
- 2 tbsp. nutritional yeast
- 2 tbsp. filtered water
- One garlic clove, peeled
- One lemon, juice extracted
- ¼ cup pine nuts
- 3 cups cauliflower, chopped

Directions:

1. Mix all fixings in a blender or food processor. Pulse until smooth.
2. Scoop into a bowl and add crushed red peppers.

Nutrition: Calories per **Serving:** 224 Carbs: 19.8g Protein: 10.5g Fat: 13.6g

Vegetarian Cabbage Rolls

Preparation Time: 5 Minutes

Cooking Time: 1 Hour and 30 Minutes

Servings: 2

Ingredients:

- One large head green cabbage
- 1 cup long-grain rice, rinsed
- Two medium zucchinis, finely diced
- 4 TB. minced garlic
- 2 tsp. salt
- 1 tsp. ground black pepper
- 4 cups plain tomato sauce
- 2 cups of water
- 1 tsp. dried mint

Directions:

1. Cut around a core of cabbage with a knife, and remove the core. Put cabbage, with core side down, in a large, 3-quart pot. Cover cabbage with water, set over high heat, and cook for 30 minutes. Drain cabbage, set aside to cool, and separate leaves. (You need 24 leaves.)
2. In a large bowl, combine long-grain rice, zucchini, one tablespoon garlic, one teaspoon salt, and 1/teaspoon black pepper.
3. In a 2-quart pot, combine tomato sauce, water, remaining tablespoons garlic, mint, remaining one teaspoon salt, and 1/2 teaspoon black pepper.
4. Lay each cabbage leaf flat on your work surface, spoon two tablespoons filling each leaf, and roll leaf.

Layer rolls in a large pot, pour the sauce into the pot, cover, and cook over medium-low heat for 1 hour.

5. Let rolls sit for 20 minutes before serving warm with Greek yogurt.

Nutrition: Calories per **Serving:** 120 Carbs: 8.0g Protein: 2.3g Fat: 9.5g

Vegan Sesame Tofu and Eggplants

Preparation Time: 5 Minutes

Cooking Time: 15 Minutes

Servings: 4

Ingredients:

- Five tablespoons olive oil
- 1-pound firm tofu, sliced
- Three tablespoons rice vinegar
- Two teaspoons Swerve sweetener
- Two whole eggplants, sliced
- ¼ cup of soy sauce
- Salt and pepper to taste
- Four tablespoons toasted sesame oil
- ¼ cup sesame seeds
- 1 cup fresh cilantro, chopped

Directions:

1. Heat the oil in a pan for 2 minutes.
2. Pan-fry the tofu for 3 minutes on each side.
3. Stir in the rice vinegar, sweetener, eggplants, and soy sauce—season with salt and pepper to taste.
4. Close the lid, then cook for around 5 minutes on medium fire. Stir and continue cooking for another 5 minutes.
5. Toss in the sesame oil, sesame seeds, and cilantro.
6. Serve and enjoy.

Nutrition: Calories per **Serving:** 616 Carbs: 27.4g Protein: 23.9g Fat: 49.2g

Steamed Squash Chowder

Preparation Time: 5 Minutes

Cooking Time: 40 Minutes

Servings: 4

Ingredients:

- 3 cups chicken broth
- 2 tbsp. ghee
- 1 tsp chili powder
- ½ tsp cumin
- 1 ½ tsp salt
- 2 tsp cinnamon
- 3 tbsp. olive oil
- Two carrots, chopped
- One small yellow onion, chopped
- One green apple, sliced and cored
- One large butternut squash

Directions:

1. In a large pot on medium-high fire, melt ghee.
2. Once the ghee is hot, sauté onions for 5 minutes or until soft and translucent.
3. Add olive oil, chili powder, cumin, salt, and cinnamon. Sauté for half a minute.
4. Add chopped squash and apples.
5. Sauté for 10 minutes while stirring once in a while.
6. Add broth, cover, and cook on medium fire for twenty minutes or until apples and squash are tender.

7. With an immersion blender, puree the chowder. Adjust consistency by adding more water.
8. Add more salt or pepper depending on desire.
9. Serve and enjoy.

Nutrition: Calories per **Serving:** 228 Carbs: 17.9g Protein: 2.2g Fat: 18.0g

Collard Green Wrap Greek Style

Preparation Time: 5 Minutes

Cooking Time: 0 Minutes

Servings: 4

Ingredients:

- ½ block feta, cut into 4 (1-inch thick) strips (4-oz)
- ½ cup purple onion, diced
- ½ medium red bell pepper, julienned
- One medium cucumber, julienned
- Four large cherry tomatoes halved
- Four large collard green leaves washed
- Eight whole kalamata olives halved
- 1 cup full-fat plain Greek yogurt
- One tablespoon white vinegar
- One teaspoon garlic powder
- Two tablespoons minced fresh dill
- Two tablespoons olive oil
- 2.5-ounces cucumber, seeded and grated (¼-whole)
- Salt and pepper to taste

Directions:

1. Make the Tzatziki sauce first: make sure to squeeze out all the excess liquid from the cucumber after grating. In a small bowl, mix all sauce fixings thoroughly and refrigerate.
2. Prepare and slice all wrap ingredients.
3. On a flat surface, spread one collard green leaf. Spread two tablespoons of Tzatziki sauce in the middle of the leaf.

4. Layer ¼ of each of the tomatoes, feta, olives, onion, pepper, and cucumber. Place them on the center of the leaf, like piling them high instead of spreading them.
5. Fold the leaf like you would a burrito. Repeat process for remaining ingredients.
6. Serve and enjoy.

Nutrition: Calories per **Serving:** 165.3 Protein: 7.0g Carbs: 9.9g Fat: 11.2g

Cayenne Eggplant Spread

Preparation Time: 5 Minutes

Cooking Time: 50 Minutes

Servings: 4

Ingredients:

- Two eggplants, trimmed
- One teaspoon cayenne pepper
- One teaspoon salt
- ½ teaspoon harissa
- One tablespoon sesame oil
- Three tablespoons Plain yogurt
- One garlic clove, peeled
- 1/3 teaspoon sumac
- One teaspoon ground paprika
- One teaspoon lemon juice

Directions:

1. Cut the eggplants on the halves and rub them with salt.
2. Preheat the oven to 375F.
3. Arrange the eggplant halves in the tray and bake them for 50 minutes.
4. When the eggplants are soft, they are ready to be used.
5. Peel the eggplants and put the peeled eggplant pulp in the blender.
6. Add cayenne pepper, harissa, sesame oil, Plain yogurt, garlic clove, sumac, and lemon juice.
7. Blend the mixture until smooth and soft.

8. Transfer the cooked meal to the serving bowls and sprinkle with ground paprika.

Nutrition: Calories 113 Fat 4.3 Fiber 10 Carbs 18 Protein 3.6

Cilantro Potato Mash

Preparation Time: 5 Minutes

Cooking Time: 20 Minutes

Servings: 2

Ingredients:

- 1 cup yam, chopped
- One tablespoon cream
- ½ teaspoon dried cilantro
- 1 cup of water
- ½ teaspoon salt

Directions:

1. Boil yum in water for 20 minutes or until it is soft.
2. Then drain the water and mash the yam with the help of the potato masher.
3. Add cream dried cilantro, and salt.
4. Mix up well.

Nutrition: Calories 92 Fat 0.5 Fiber 3.1 Carbs 21.1 Protein 1.2

Cheese and Broccoli Balls

Preparation Time: 5 Minutes

Cooking Time: 5 Minutes

Servings: 4

Ingredients:

- ¾ cup almond flour
- Two large eggs
- Two teaspoons baking powder
- 4 ounces fresh broccoli
- 4 ounces mozzarella cheese
- Seven tablespoons flaxseed meal
- Salt and Pepper to taste
- ¼ cup fresh chopped dill
- ¼ cup mayonnaise
- ½ tablespoon lemon juice
- Salt and pepper to taste

Directions:

1. Place broccoli in the food processor and pulse into small pieces. Transfer to a bowl.
2. Add ¼ cup flaxseed meal, baking powder, almond flour, and cheese. Season with pepper and salt if desired. Mix well—place remaining flaxseed meal in a small bowl.
3. Add eggs and combine thoroughly. Roll the batter into 1-inch balls. Then roll in flaxseed meal to hide the balls.

4. Cook balls in a 3750F deep-fryer until golden brown, about 5 minutes. Transfer cooked balls on to a paper towel-lined plate.
5. In the meantime, make the sauce by combining all fixings in a medium bowl.
6. Serve cheese and broccoli balls with the plunging sauce on the side.

Nutrition: Calories per **Serving:** 312 Protein: 18.4g Carbs: 9.6g Fat: 23.2g

Hot Pepper Sauce

Preparation Time: 10 Minutes

Cooking Time: 20 Minutes

Servings: 4 Cups

Ingredients:

- Two red hot fresh chiles, deseeded
- Two dried chiles
- Two garlic cloves, peeled
- ½ small yellow onion, roughly chopped
- 2 cups of water
- 2 cups white vinegar

Directions:

1. Place all the fixings except the vinegar in a medium saucepan over medium heat. Allow simmering for 20 minutes until softened.
2. Transfer the combination to a food processor or blender. Stir in the vinegar and pulse until very smooth.
3. Serve instantly or transfer to a sealed container and refrigerate for up to 3 months.

Nutrition: Calories: 20 Fat: 1.2g Protein: 0.6g Carbs: 4.4g Fiber: 0.6g Sodium: 12mg

Lemon-Tahini Sauce

Preparation Time: 10 Minutes

Cooking Time: 0 Minutes

Servings: 1 Cup

Ingredients:

- ½ cup tahini
- One garlic clove, minced
- Juice and zest of 1 lemon
- ½ teaspoon salt, plus more as needed
- ½ cup warm water, plus more as needed

Directions:

1. Combine the tahini and garlic in a small bowl.
2. Add the lemon juice and zest, and salt to the bowl and stir to mix well.
3. Fold in the warm water and whisk until well combined and creamy. Feel free to add more warm water if you like a thinner consistency.
4. Taste and add additional salt as needed.
5. Stock the sauce in a sealed vessel in the refrigerator for up to 5 days.

Nutrition: Calories: 179 Fat: 15.5g Protein: 5.1g Carbs: 6.8g Fiber: 3.0g Sodium: 324mg

Peri-Peri Sauce

Preparation Time: 10 Minutes

Cooking Time: 5 Minutes

Servings: 4

Ingredients:

- One tomato, chopped
- One red onion, chopped
- One red bell pepper, deseeded and chopped
- One red chile, deseeded and chopped
- Four garlic cloves, minced
- Two tablespoons extra-virgin olive oil
- Juice of 1 lemon
- One tablespoon dried oregano
- One tablespoon smoked paprika
- One teaspoon sea salt

Directions:

1. Process all the fixings in a food processor or a blender until smooth.
2. Transfer the mixture to a small saucepan over medium-high heat and bring to a boil, stirring often.
3. Decrease the heat to medium and let to simmer for 5 minutes until heated through.
4. You can store the sauce in an airtight container in the refrigerator for up to 5 days.

Nutrition: Calories: 98 Fat: 6.5g Protein: 1.0g Carbs: 7.8g Fiber: 3.0g Sodium: 295mg

Peanut Sauce with Honey

Preparation Time: 5 Minutes

Cooking Time: 0 Minutes

Servings: 4

Ingredients:

- ¼ cup peanut butter
- One tablespoon peeled and grated fresh ginger
- One tablespoon honey
- One tablespoon low-sodium soy sauce
- One garlic clove, minced
- Juice of 1 lime
- Pinch red pepper flakes

Directions:

1. Whisk together all the fixings in a small bowl until well incorporated.
2. Transfer to an airtight vessel and refrigerate for up to 5 days.

Nutrition: Calories: 117 Fat: 7.6g Protein: 4.1g Carbs: 8.8g Fiber: 1.0g Sodium: 136mg

Cilantro-Tomato Salsa

Preparation Time: 10 Minutes

Cooking Time: 0 Minutes

Servings: 6

Ingredients:

- 2 or 3 medium, ripe tomatoes, diced
- One serrano pepper, seeded and minced
- ½ red onion, minced
- ¼ cup minced fresh cilantro
- Juice of 1 lime
- ¼ teaspoon salt, plus more as needed

Directions:

1. Place the tomatoes, serrano pepper, onion, cilantro, lime juice, and salt in a small bowl and mix well.
2. Taste and add additional salt, if needed.
3. Stock in an airtight vessel in the refrigerator for up to 3 days.

Nutrition: Calories: 17 Fat: 0g Protein: 1.0g Carbs: 3.9g Fiber: 1.0g Sodium: 83mg

Cheesy Pea Pesto

Preparation Time: 5 Minutes

Cooking Time: 0 Minutes

Servings: 4

Ingredients:

- ½ cup fresh green peas
- ½ cup grated Parmesan cheese
- ¼ cup extra-virgin olive oil
- ¼ cup pine nuts
- ¼ cup fresh basil leaves
- Two garlic cloves, minced
- ¼ teaspoon of sea salt

Directions:

1. Add all the fixings to a food processor or blender and pulse until the nuts are chopped finely.
2. Transfer to an airtight vessel and refrigerate for up to 2 days. You can also stock it in ice cube trays in the freezer for up to 6 months.

Nutrition: Calories: 247 Fat: 22.8g Protein: 7.1g Carbs: 4.8g Fiber: 1.0g Sodium: 337mg

Guacamole

Preparation Time: 10 Minutes

Cooking Time: 0 Minutes

Servings: 6

Ingredients:
- Two large avocados
- ¼ white onion, finely diced
- One small, firm tomato, finely diced
- ¼ cup finely chopped fresh cilantro
- Two tablespoons freshly squeezed lime juice
- ¼ teaspoon salt
- Freshly ground black pepper, to taste

Directions:
1. Cut the avocados in half and take away the pits. Using a large spoon to scoop out the flesh and add to a medium bowl.
2. Puree the avocado flesh with the back of a fork or until a uniform consistency is achieved. Add the onion, tomato, cilantro, lime juice, salt, and pepper to the bowl and stir to combine.
3. Serve instantly or transfer to an airtight container and refrigerate until chilled.

Nutrition: Calories: 81 Fat: 6.8g Protein: 1.1g Carbs: 5.7g Fiber: 3.0g Sodium: 83mg

Simple Italian Dressing

Preparation Time: 5 Minutes

Cooking Time: 0 Minutes

Servings: 12

Ingredients:

- ½ cup extra-virgin olive oil
- ¼ cup red wine vinegar
- One teaspoon dried Italian seasoning
- One teaspoon Dijon mustard
- ¼ teaspoon salt
- ¼ teaspoon freshly ground black pepper
- One garlic clove, minced

Directions:

1. Place all the fixings in a mason jar and cover.
2. Shake vigorously for 1 minute until thoroughly mixed.
3. Stock in the fridge for up to 1 week.

Nutrition: Calories: 80 Fat: 8.6g Protein: 0g Carbs: 0g Fiber: 0g Sodium: 51mg

Ranch-Style Cauliflower Dressing

Preparation Time: 10 Minutes

Cooking Time: 0 Minutes

Servings: 8

Ingredients:

- 2 cups frozen cauliflower, thawed
- ½ cup unsweetened plain almond milk
- Two tablespoons apple cider vinegar
- Two tablespoons extra-virgin olive oil
- One garlic clove, peeled
- Two teaspoons finely chopped fresh parsley
- Two teaspoons finely chopped scallions (both white and green parts)
- One teaspoon finely chopped fresh dill
- ½ teaspoon onion powder
- ½ teaspoon Dijon mustard
- ½ teaspoon salt
- ¼ teaspoon freshly ground black pepper

Directions:

1. Place all the fixings in a blender and pulse until creamy and smooth.
2. Serve instantly, or transfer to an airtight container to refrigerate for up to 3 days.

Nutrition: Calories: 41 Fat: 3.6g Protein: 1.0g Carbs: 1.9g Fiber: 1.1g Sodium: 148mg

Asian-Inspired Vinaigrette

Preparation Time: 5 Minutes

Cooking Time: 0 Minutes

Servings: 2

Ingredients:

- 1/4 cup extra-virgin olive oil
- Three tablespoons apple cider vinegar
- One garlic clove, minced
- One tablespoon peeled and grated fresh ginger
- One tablespoon chopped fresh cilantro
- One tablespoon freshly squeezed lime juice
- ½ teaspoon sriracha

Directions:

1. Add all the fixings to a small bowl and stir to mix well.
2. Serve immediately, or store covered in the refrigerator and shake before using.

Nutrition: Calories: 251 Fat: 26.8g Protein: 0g Carbs: 1.8g Fiber: 0.7g Sodium: 3mg

Parsley Vinaigrette

Preparation Time: 5 Minutes

Cooking Time: 0 Minutes

Servings: ½ Cup

Ingredients:

- ½ cup lightly packed fresh parsley, finely chopped
- 1/3 cup extra-virgin olive oil
- Three tablespoons red wine vinegar
- One garlic clove, minced
- ¼ teaspoon salt, plus additional as needed

Directions:

1. Place all the fixings in a mason jar and cover. Shake vigorously for 1 minute until completely mixed.
2. Taste and add additional salt as needed.
3. Serve immediately or serve chilled.

Nutrition: Calories: 92 Fat: 10.9g Protein: 0g Carbs: 0g Fiber: 0g Sodium: 75mg

Homemade Blackened Seasoning

Preparation Time: 10 Minutes

Cooking Time: 0 Minutes

Servings: ½ Cup

Ingredients:

- Two tablespoons smoked paprika
- Two tablespoons garlic powder
- Two tablespoons onion powder
- One tablespoon sweet paprika
- One teaspoon dried dill
- One teaspoon freshly ground black pepper
- ½ teaspoon ground mustard
- ¼ teaspoon celery seeds

Directions:

1. Add all the fixings to a small bowl and mix well.
2. Serve immediately, or put in an airtight container and store in a cool, dry, and dark place for up to 3 months.

Nutrition: Calories: 22 Fat: 0.9g Protein: 1.0g Carbs: 4.7g Fiber: 1.0g Sodium: 2mg

Not Old Bay Seasoning

Preparation Time: 10 Minutes

Cooking Time: 0 Minutes

Servings: ½ Cup

Ingredients:

- Three tablespoons sweet paprika
- One tablespoon mustard seed
- Two tablespoons celery seeds
- Two teaspoons freshly ground black pepper
- 1½ teaspoons cayenne pepper
- One teaspoon red pepper flake
- ½ teaspoon ground ginger
- ½ teaspoon ground nutmeg
- ½ teaspoon ground cinnamon
- ¼ teaspoon ground cloves

Directions:

1. Mix all the fixings in an airtight container until well combined.
2. You can keep it in a dry, cool, and dark place for up to 3 months.

Nutrition: Calories: 26 Fat: 1.9g Protein: 1.1g Carbs: 3.6g Fiber: 2.1g Sodium: 3mg

Creamy Cucumber Dip

Preparation Time: 10 Minutes

Cooking Time: 0 Minutes

Servings: 6

Ingredients:

- One medium cucumber, peeled and grated
- ¼ teaspoon salt
- 1 cup plain Greek yogurt
- Two garlic cloves, minced
- One tablespoon extra-virgin olive oil
- One tablespoon freshly squeezed lemon juice
- ¼ teaspoon freshly ground black pepper

Directions:

1. Put the grated cucumber in a colander set over a bowl, and season with salt. Allow the cucumber to sit for 10 minutes. Using your hands, squash out as much liquid from the cucumber as possible. Transfer the grated cucumber to a bowl.
2. Add the yogurt, garlic, olive oil, lemon juice, and pepper to the bowl and stir until well blended.
3. Cover the bowl with plastic wrap. Keep it in the freezer for approximately 2 hours to blend the flavors.
4. Serve chilled.

Nutrition: Calories: 47 Fat: 2.8g Protein: 4.2g Carbs: 2.7g Fiber: 0g Sodium: 103mg

Lentil-Tahini Dip

Preparation Time: 10 Minutes

Cooking Time: 15 Minutes

Servings: 3 Cups

Ingredients:

- 1 cup dried green or brown lentils
- 2½ cups water, divided
- 1/3 cup tahini
- One garlic clove
- ½ teaspoon salt, plus more as needed

Directions:

1. Pour the lentils and 2 cups of water into a medium saucepan and bring to a boil over high heat.
2. Once it twitches to boil, reduce the heat to low, and then cook for 14 minutes, stirring occasionally, or the lentils become tender but still hold their shape. You can drain any excess liquid.
3. Handover the lentils to a food processor and the remaining water, tahini, garlic, salt, and process until smooth and creamy.
4. Taste and adjust the seasoning if needed. Serve immediately.

Nutrition: Calories: 100 Fat: 3.9g Protein: 5.1g Carbs: 10.7g Fiber: 6.0g Sodium: 106mg

Pistachio Arugula Salad

Preparation Time: 20 minutes

Cooking Time: 0 minute

Serving: 6

Size/ Portion: 2 cups

Ingredients:

- ¼ cup olive oil
- 6 cups kale, chopped rough
- 2 cups arugula
- ½ teaspoon smoked paprika
- 2 tablespoons lemon juice, fresh
- 1/3 cup pistachios, unsalted & shelled
- 6 tablespoons parmesan, grated

Directions:

1. Get out a large bowl and combine your oil, lemon juice, kale and smoked paprika. Massage it into the leaves for about fifteen seconds. You then need to allow it to sit for ten minutes.
2. Mix everything together before serving with grated cheese on top.

Nutrition: 150 Calories 5g Protein 12g Fat

Potato Salad

Preparation Time: 9 minutes

Cooking Time: 13 minutes

Serving: 6

Size/ Portion: 2 cups

Ingredients:

- 2 lbs. golden potatoes

- 3 tablespoons olive oil

- 3 tablespoons lemon juice, fresh

- 1 tablespoon olive brine

- ¼ teaspoon sea salt, fine

- ½ cup olives, sliced

- 1 cup celery, sliced

- 2 tablespoons oregano

- 2 tablespoons mint leaves

Directions:

1. Boil potatoes in saucepan before turning the heat down to medium-low. Cook for fifteen more minutes.

2. Get out a small bowl and whisk your oil, lemon juice, olive brine and salt together.

3. Drain your potatoes using a colander and transfer it to a serving bowl. Pour in three tablespoons of dressing over your potatoes, and mix well with oregano, and min along with the remaining dressing.

Nutrition: 175 Calories 3g Protein 7g Fat

Raisin Rice Pilaf

Preparation Time: 13 minutes

Cooking Time: 8 minutes

Serving: 5

Size/ Portion: 2 cups

Ingredients:

- 1 tablespoon olive oil

- 1 teaspoon cumin

- 1 cup onion, chopped

- ½ cup carrot, shredded

- ½ teaspoon cinnamon

- 2 cups instant brown rice

- 1 ¾ cup orange juice

- 1 cup golden raisins

- ¼ cup water

- ½ cup pistachios, shelled

- fresh chives, chopped for garnish

Directions:

1. Place a medium saucepan over medium-high heat before adding in your oil. Add n your onion, and stir often so it doesn't burn. Cook for about five minutes

and then add in your cumin, cinnamon and carrot. Cook for about another minute.

2. Add in your orange juice, water and rice. Boil before covering your saucepan. Turn the heat down to medium-low and then allow it to simmer for six to seven minutes.

3. Stir in your pistachios, chives and raisins. Serve warm.

Nutrition: 320 Calories 6g Protein 7g Fat

Lebanese Delight

Preparation Time: 7 minutes

Cooking Time: 25 minutes

Serving: 5

Size/ Portion: 2 ounces

Ingredients:

- 1 tablespoon olive oil

- 1 cup vermicelli

- 3 cups cabbage, shredded

- 3 cups vegetable broth, low sodium

- ½ cup water

- 1 cup instant brown rice

- ¼ teaspoon sea salt, fine

- 2 cloves garlic

- ¼ teaspoon crushed red pepper

- ½ cup cilantro fresh & chopped

- lemon slices to garnish

Directions:

1. Get out a saucepan and then place it over medium-high heat. Add in your oil and once it's hot you will need to add in your pasta. Cook for three minutes or

until your pasta is toasted. You will have to stir often in order to keep it from burning.

2. Ad in your cabbage, cooking for another four minutes. Continue to stir often.

3. Add in your water and rice. Season with salt, red pepper and garlic before bringing it all to a boil over high heat. Stir, and then cover. Once it's covered turn the heat down to medium-low. Allow it all to simmer for ten minutes.

4. Remove the pan from the burner and then allow it to sit without lifting the lid for five minutes. Take the garlic cloves out and then mash them using a fork. Place them back in, and stir them into the rice. Stir in your cilantro as well and serve warm. Garnish with lemon wedges if desired.

Nutrition: 259 Calories 7g Protein 4g Fat

Mediterranean Sweet Potato

Preparation Time: 6 minutes

Cooking Time: 25 minutes

Serving: 4

Size/ Portion: 1 cup

Ingredients:

- 4 sweet potatoes
- 15 ounce can chickpeas, rinsed & drained
- ½ tablespoon olive oil
- ½ teaspoon cumin
- ½ teaspoon coriander
- ½ teaspoon cinnamon
- 1 pinch sea salt, fine
- ½ teaspoon paprika
- ¼ cup hummus
- 1 tablespoon lemon juice, fresh
- 2-3 teaspoon dill, fresh
- 3 cloves garlic, minced
- unsweetened almond milk as needed

Directions:

1. Set oven to 400, and then get out a baking sheet. Line it with foil.

2. Wash your sweet potatoes before halving them lengthwise.

3. Take your olive oil, cumin, chickpeas, coriander, sea salt and paprika on your baking sheet. Rub the sweet potatoes with olive oil, placing them face down over the mixture.

4. Roast for twenty to twenty-five minutes.

5. Mix your dill, lemon juice, hummus, garlic and a dash of almond milk.

6. Smash the insides of the sweet potato down, topping with chickpea mixture and sauce before serving.

Nutrition: 313 Calories 8.6g Protein 9g fats

Flavorful Braised Kale

Preparation Time: 7 minutes

Cooking Time: 32 minutes

Serving: 6

Size/ Portion: 1 cup

Ingredients:

- 1 lb. Kale
- 1 Cup Cherry Tomatoes, Halved
- 2 Teaspoons Olive Oil
- 4 Cloves Garlic, Sliced Thin
- ½ Cup Vegetable Stock
- ¼ Teaspoon Sea Salt, Fine
- 1 Tablespoon Lemon Juice, Fresh
- 1/8 Teaspoon Black Pepper

Directions:

1. Preheat olive oil in a frying pan using medium heat, and add in your garlic. Sauté for a minute or two until lightly golden.

2. Mix your kale and vegetable stock with your garlic, adding it to your pan.

3. Cover the pan and then turn the heat down to medium-low.

4. Allow it to cook until your kale wilts and part of your vegetable stock should be dissolved.

5. Stir in your tomatoes and cook without a lid until your kale is tender, and then remove it from heat.

6. Mix in your salt, pepper and lemon juice before serving warm.

Nutrition: 70 Calories 4g Protein 0.5g Fat

Bean Salad

Preparation Time: 16 minutes

Cooking Time: 0 minutes

Serving: 6

Size/ Portion: 2 ounces

Ingredients:

- 1 can garbanzo beans, rinsed & drained
- 2 tablespoons balsamic vinegar
- ¼ cup olive oil
- 4 cloves garlic, chopped fine
- 1/3 cup parsley, fresh & chopped
- ¼ cup olive oil
- 1 red onion, diced
- 6 lettuce leaves
- ½ cup celery, chopped fine/black pepper to taste

Directions:

1. Make the vinaigrette dressing by whipping together your garlic, parsley, vinegar and pepper in a bowl.

2. Add the olive oil to this mixture and whisk before setting it aside.

3. Add in your onion and beans, and then pour your dressing on top. Toss then cover it. Chill before serving

4. Place a lettuce leaf on the plate when serving and spoon the mixture in. garnish with celery.

Nutrition: 218 Calories 7g Protein 0.1g Fat

Basil Tomato Skewers

Preparation Time: 14 minutes

Cooking Time: 0 minute

Serving: 2

Size/ Portion: 1 skewer

Ingredients:

- 16 mozzarella balls, fresh & small

- 16 basil leaves, fresh

- 16 cherry tomatoes

- olive oil to drizzle

- sea salt & black pepper to taste

Directions:

1. Start by threading your basil, cheese and tomatoes together on small skewers.

2. Drizzle with oil before seasoning. Serve.

Nutrition: 46 Calories 7.6g Protein 0.9g Fat

Olives with Feta

Preparation Time: 5 minutes

Cooking Time: 0 minute

Serving: 4

Size/ Portion: 1

Ingredients:

- ½ Cup Feta Cheese
- 1 Cup Kalamata Olives
- 2 Cloves Garlic, Sliced
- 2 Tablespoons Olive Oil
- 1 Lemon, Zested & Juiced
- 1 Teaspoon Rosemary, Fresh & Chopped
- Crushed Red Pepper
- Black Pepper to Taste

Directions:

1. Mix everything together and serve over crackers.

Nutrition: 71 Calories 4g Protein 2.6g Fat

Black Bean Medley

Preparation Time: 5 minutes

Cooking Time: 0 minute

Serving: 4

Size/ Portion: 1 cup

Ingredients:

- 4 plum tomatoes, chopped

- 14.5 ounces black beans, canned & drained

- ½ red onion, sliced

- ¼ cup dill, fresh & chopped

- 1 lemon, juiced

- 2 tablespoons olive oil

- ¼ cup feta cheese, crumbled

- sea salt to taste

Directions:

1. Mix everything in a bowl except for your feta and salt. Top the beans with salt and feta.

Nutrition: 121 Calories 6g Protein 5g Fat

Mediterranean Quiche

Preparation Time: 7 minutes

Cooking Time: 25 minutes

Serving: 6

Size/ Portion: 1 slice

Ingredients

- ½ cup sundried tomatoes
- 2 cloves garlic, minced
- 1 onion, diced
- 2 tablespoons butter
- 1 prepared pie crust
- boiling water
- 1 red pepper, diced
- 2 cups spinach, fresh
- ¼ cup kalamata olives
- 1 teaspoon oregano
- 1 teaspoon parsley
- 1/3 cup feta cheese, crumbled
- 4 eggs, large
- 1 ¼ cup milk

- sea salt & black pepper to taste

- 1 cup cheddar cheese, shredded & divided

Directions:

1. Add your tomatoes to boiling water and allow it to cook for five minutes before draining.

2. Chop the tomatoes before setting them to the side, and adjust the oven to 375.

3. Spread the pie crust into a nine-inch pie pan, and heat the butter and add in your garlic and onion.

4. Cook for three minutes before adding in your red pepper, and then cook for another three minutes.

5. Add in your parsley and oregano before adding in your spinach and olives. Cook for about another five minutes. Take it off heat, and then add in your feta cheese and tomatoes.

6. Spread your mixture into the prepared pie crust, and then beat the egg and milk. Season with salt and pepper and then add in half a cup of cheese.

7. Pour this mixture over your spinach, and then bake for fifty-five minutes. It should be golden, and serve warm.

Nutrition: 417 Calories 14.5g Protein 13.3g Fat

Grilled Fish with Lemons

Preparation Time: 8 minutes

Cooking Time: 20 minutes

Serving: 4

Size/ Portion: 1 piece

Ingredients:

- 3-4 Lemons

- 1 Tablespoon Olive Oil

- Sea Salt & Black Pepper to Taste

- 4 Catfish Fillets, 4 Ounces Each

- Nonstick Cooking Spray

Directions:

1. Pat your fillets dry using a paper towel and let them come to room temperature. This may take ten minutes. Coat the cooking grate of your grill with nonstick cooking spray while it's cold. Once it's coated preheat it to 400 degrees.

2. Cut one lemon in half, setting it to the side. Slice your remaining half of the lemon into ¼ inch slices. Get out a bowl and squeeze a tablespoon of juice from your reserved half. Add your oil to the bowl, mixing well.

3. Brush your fish down with the oil and lemon mixture.

4. Place your lemon slices on the grill and then put our fillets on top. Grill with your lid closed. Turn the fish halfway through if they're more than a half an inch thick.

Nutrition: 147 Calories 22g Protein 1g Fat

Pesto Walnut Noodles

Preparation Time: 7 minutes

Cooking Time: 25 minutes

Serving: 4

Size/ Portion: 2 ounces

Ingredients:

- 4 Zucchini, Made into Zoodles

- ¼ Cup Olive Oil, Divided

- ½ Teaspoon Crushed Red Pepper

- 2 Cloves Garlic, Minced & Divided

- ¼ Teaspoon Black Pepper

- ¼ Teaspoon sea Salt

- 2 Tablespoons Parmesan Cheese, Grated & Divided

- 1 Cup Basil, Fresh & Packed

- ¾ Cup Walnut Pieces, Divided

Directions:

1. Start by making your zucchini noodles by using a spiralizer to get ribbons. Combine your zoodles with a minced garlic clove and tablespoon of oil. Season with salt and pepper and crushed red pepper. Set it to the side.

2. Get out a large skillet and heat a ½ a tablespoon of oil over medium-high heat. Add in half of your zoodles, cooking for five minutes. Repeat with another ½ a tablespoon of oil and your remaining zoodles.

3. Make your pesto while your zoodles cook. Put your garlic clove, a tablespoon or parmesan, basil leaves and ¼ cup of walnuts in your food processor. Season with salt and pepper if desired, and drizzle the remaining two tablespoons of oil in until completely blended.

4. Add the pesto to your zoodles, topping with remaining walnuts and parmesan to serve.

Nutrition: 301 Calories 7g Protein 28g Fat

Tomato Tabbouleh

Preparation Time: 6 minutes

Cooking Time: 30 minutes

Serving: 4

Size/ Portion: 1 cup

Ingredients:

- 8 beefsteak tomatoes
- ½ cup water
- 3 tablespoons olive oil, divided
- ½ cup whole wheat couscous, uncooked
- 1 ½ cups parsley, fresh & minced
- 2 scallions chopped
- 1/3 cup mint, fresh & minced
- sea salt & black pepper to taste
- 1 lemon
- 4 teaspoons honey, raw
- 1/3 cup almonds, chopped

Directions:

1. Set oven to 400 degrees. Take your tomato and slice the top off each one before scooping the flesh out. Put the tops flesh and seeds in a mixing bowl.

2. Get out a baking dish before adding in a tablespoon of oil to grease it. Place your tomatoes in the dish, and then cover your dish with foil.

3. Now you will make your couscous while your tomatoes cook. Bring the water to a boil using a saucepan and then add the couscous in and cover. Remove it from heat, and allow it to sit for five minutes. Fluff it with a fork.

4. Chop your tomato flesh and tops up, and then drain the excess water using a colander. Measure a cup of your chopped tomatoes and place them back in the mixing bowl. Mix with mint scallions, pepper, salt and parsley.

5. Zest lemon, and then half the lemon. Squeeze the lemon juice in, and mix well.

6. Add your tomato mix to the couscous.

7. Carefully remove your tomatoes from the oven and then divide your tabbouleh among your tomatoes. Cover the pan with foil and then put it in the oven. Cook for another eight to ten minutes.

8. Drizzle with honey and top with almonds before serving.

Nutrition: 314 Calories 8g Protein 15g Fat

Lemon Faro Bowl

Preparation Time: 9 minutes

Cooking Time: 25 minutes

Serving: 6

Size/ Portion: 2 cups

Ingredients:

- 1 ½ tablespoon olive oil

- 1 cup onion, chopped

- 2 cloves garlic, minced

- 1 carrot, shredded

- 2 cups vegetable broth, low sodium

- 1 cup pearled faro

- 2 avocados, peeled, pitted & sliced

- 1 lemon, small

Directions:

1. Situate saucepan over medium-high heat. Add in a tablespoon of oil and then throw in your onion once the oil is hot. Cook for about five minutes, stirring frequently to keep it from burning.

2. Add in your carrot and garlic. Allow it to cook for about another minute while you continue to stir.

3. Add in your broth and faro. Boil and adjust your heat to high to help. Once it boils, lower it to medium-low and cover your saucepan. Let it simmer for twenty minutes.

4. Pour the faro into a bowl and add in your avocado and zest. Drizzle with your remaining oil and add in your lemon wedges.

Nutrition: 279 Calories 7g Protein 14g Fat

Conclusion

The Mediterranean diet considers various aspects of what "health" means. It does not just focus on what you eat but it also focuses on how you eat, who you eat with, and the activities you do in between eating. Each of these components can contribute to better health and a more fulfilling life. When we are lacking in any of these components, we tend to suffer from poor health, fatigue, depression and more. The Mediterranean diet was originally looked at because of its heart health benefits, but now it is clear to see that the traditional Mediterranean lifestyle from the 1950s was more than just a heart-healthy plan.

This book has helped you understand not only the benefits of this diet but has revealed effective tips and suggestions to help you transition into this type of diet. The changes can be made in small steps, because even the smallest change to shifting your diet to a more Mediterranean diet can have a whirlwind of benefits. You have learned how to swap the unhealthy foods you have been used to consuming with nutrient-dense and wholesome foods.

The Mediterranean diet is more than what you eat; it is a way of living. This diet reflects the true definition of what a diet should be. It encourages eating healthy nutritious foods, while also emphasizing the importance of physical activity and spending time with those we care about. The Mediterranean diet has been studied for decades and each time it seems a new benefit of this diet comes to light.

What needs to be done is adopting a new way of looking at food and mealtimes. Our world today stresses working harder and longer which means there is little time for enjoying meals. If we can change our perspective to see that the food, we eat is what makes us more efficient and productive, then we would be able to more easily change the way we eat.

This book has introduced you to what the Mediterranean diet is. It has helped you understand that this isn't your typical diet. That instead, the Mediterranean diet is about changing into a lifestyle that will bring you better health and happiness. This book has provided you with some of the findings from scientific research that supports the diet's benefits. You have learned that the diet consists of eating plenty of fresh fruits, vegetables, and healthy fats like extra virgin olive oil. You still have the freedom to indulge with brain-boosting fish, heart-healthy whole grains, and seafood and sporadically can enjoy a nice steak dinner. This diet is not limiting you to be mindful of your calorie intake or not to consume other important food groups.

The recipes in this book allow you to begin trying out delicious, flavorful, and healthy Mediterranean inspired meals. You have a number of breakfasts, lunch, and dinner options that are sure to satisfy and please everyone in your home. These recipes c be your starting point in taking control of your health.

You now have a better understanding that this diet is not about just losing weight. It is not a diet that allows you to eat your weight in pasta, or drink equal amounts of red wine. It has shown that you can use food as a form of natural medicine to reduce and eliminate the risk of many serious health conditions. You have learned how your food directly affects the way your body functions and when it is deprived of the nutrients it needs it will not be able to perform appropriately.

Now that you have all this information on how you can maintain and achieve optimal health, it is up to you to decide. Will you continue to choose a life where the foods you eat leads you down a road to illness and preventable suffering? Or will you make the change now to live your life and be the healthiest and happiest version of you? All you have to do is start with one small change and then go from there. Once you begin to see the benefits from that one small choice you will be eager to try more and soon you will be living a Mediterranean lifestyle that is significantly more satisfying.

Finally, this book was intended to assist you recognize that diet does not need to make you give up some of your beloved foods. Instead, it allows you to find new favorites that will improve your overall health. Allow the food you enjoy today to be your medicine for your future.

CPSIA information can be obtained
at www.ICGtesting.com
Printed in the USA
BVHW092243260421
605885BV00002B/213